THE LITTLE GIANT® BOOK OF

SCHOOL
JOKES

CHARLES KELLER

ILLUSTRATED BY JEFF SINCLAIR

Sterling Publishing Co., Inc.
New York

To Brenda Gordon

I would like to acknowledge the help of Marcus Bocchino and Rhoda Crispell.

Library of Congress Cataloging-in-Publication Data Available

10   9   8   7   6   5   4   3   2   1

Published by Sterling Publishing Company, Inc.
387 Park Avenue South, New York, N.Y. 10016
© 2000 by Charles Keller
Distributed in Canada by Sterling Publishing
c/o Canadian Manda Group, One Atlantic Avenue, Suite 105
Toronto, Ontario, Canada M6K 3E7
Distributed in Great Britain and Europe by Chris Lloyd
463 Ashley Road, Parkstone, Poole, Dorset, BH14 0AX, England
Distributed in Australia by Capricorn Link (Australia) Pty Ltd.
P.O. Box 6651, Baulkham Hills, Business Centre, NSW 2153,
Australia
Manufactured in Canada
All rights reserved

Sterling ISBN 0-8069-0469-0

Contents

MAKING THE GRADE

Why didn't the school alarm go off in time?

It was a dumb bell.

A first grader slipped in the hall in
school and skinned his knee. A
teacher came up to him, examined
his knee, and said, "Remember, big
boys don't cry." The boy answered,
"I'm not going to cry. I'm going to
sue."

6

Why did the school bell think it was engaged?

Someone gave it a ring.

TEACHER: We start school exactly at eight o'clock.

PUPIL: That's okay with me, but if I'm not here by then just go ahead and start without me.

What did you learn your first day in school?

Not much. I have to go again tomorrow.

When does school usually begin?
Too soon.

Why are school buses yellow?
Because they ran out of purple.

How did the bumble bee get to school?
It took the school buzz.

STUDENT: I couldn't get to school because I started too late.
TEACHER: Then why didn't you start earlier?
STUDENT: It was too late to start early.

BOOK NEVER WRITTEN

Why the Girl Walked to School, by Mister Bus

What's the difference between a school bus driver and a cold?
One knows the stops and the other stops the nose.

How do we know school buses are afraid?
They're yellow.

Where do small intestines go to school?
Kidney-garten.

Where did the fireplace go to school?
Kindle-garten.

What's the best place to grow
flowers in school?
  In the kinder-garden.

What do construction workers play
with in kindergarten?
Building blocks.

How do you mail the alphabet?
In a letter box.

What would you get if you crossed the alphabet with a top?

Dizzy spells.

Why did the policeman study the alphabet?

To follow the letter of the law.

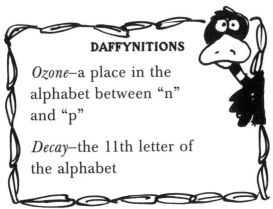

DAFFYNITIONS

Ozone–a place in the alphabet between "n" and "p"

Decay–the 11th letter of the alphabet

What letter comes after "A"?
All the others.

What comes after "G"?
Whiz.

Then what comes after "O"?
Yeah.

LARRY: What is the first letter in
   "yellow"?
HARRY: "Y".
LARRY: Because I want to know.

Why did the blackboard get mad at
school?
   It got rubbed the wrong way.

What happened when the investor
put all his money into erasers?
   He was wiped out.

TEACHER: Haven't you finished
cleaning the blackboard yet?
STUDENT: Not yet. The more I
clean, the blacker it gets.

How do blackboards start over?
With a clean slate.

What did one blackboard say to the other?
"E-rase you to the corner."

Who invented the first pen?
The Incas.

TOM SWIFTIES

"I just sharpened 12 pencils," said Tom pointlessly.

"My pencil broke," Tom snapped.

What's the difference between a pen and a pencil?

You push a pen but a pencil must be lead.

Why is the pen mightier than the sword?

No one ever invented a ballpoint sword.

What's the difference between a bird-watcher and a bad speller?

One watches birds and the other botches words.

What kind of bee drops its honey?
A spilling bee.

I got an "A" in spelling.
Silly, there is no "A" in spelling.

MOTHER: My child is a genius. She has the most original ideas, hasn't she?
TEACHER: Yes, especially when it comes to spelling.

Why was the witch first in her class?
She was a good speller.

What's a synonym?
A word you use when you can't spell the other word.

Why didn't the bowling pins go to school?

They were on strike.

What's the best part of the school year?

Summer vacation.

TEACHER: What's your favorite state?

STUDENT: Mississippi.

TEACHER: Spell it.

STUDENT: I changed my mind. It's Ohio.

TEACHER: Spell "cattle."

FRED: C-A-T-T-T-L-E.

TEACHER: Leave out one of the "T"'s.

FRED: Which one?

Why didn't the skeleton like to go to school?

His heart wasn't in it.

What exercise makes you miss
school?
Skipping.

Have you missed school lately?
Not a bit.

24

Do you like going to school?

Yes, I like to come home too. It's the staying there in between that I don't like.

When is attendance at school like a gift?

When you're present.

Well, how do you like school?

Closed.

How far did you go in school?

About three miles.

Why did the beautician go to school?
*The teacher was giving a make-up
exam.*

Why did the skeleton go to school?
To bone up on a few things.

What golf equipment was out when attendance was taken?

Absent-tees.

Why did the captain miss school?

Because he was a skipper.

Why did the kids get wet going to school?

They were in a carpool.

Why did the entertainer go to school?

He had a class act.

Why did the chicken go to school?
For eggstra credit.

Why did the teacher take away the
student's scissors?
She didn't want him to cut class.

28

Why did Cyclops give up teaching?
He only had one pupil.

Why did the teacher bring honey to school?
She wanted bee students.

What's a teacher?
One who uses marking pens for penning marks.

What do you call it when your father has to take a test?
A pop quiz.

How did the card do on the finals?
It aced them.

Teacher, I don't think I deserve a zero on this test.

Neither do I, but it's the lowest mark I can think of.

STUDENT: I have a question.

TEACHER: What is it?

STUDENT: If light travels at 186,000 miles per second, how come it goes so slowly when we're in school?

JOEY: My Sunday school teacher says that we are on earth to help other people.

MOTHER: Of course.

JOEY: Then what are the other people here on earth for?

What do batteries study for?
The acid test.

How did you make out in school?
Did you pass?
No, but I was almost at the top of
the list of failures.

Did you finish that paper in school? The one where you had to name the nine greatest world figures?

Uh, almost. I still haven't decided on a first baseman.

TEACHER: Is there anything you can do better than anyone else?
STUDENT: Yes, read my own handwriting.

What sickness do you get when you're tired of school?

Class-trophobia.

LACK OF CLASS

Why did the lettuce study so hard?
It wanted to be at the head of its class.

Why were everyone's grades slanted?

The teacher marked on a curve.

What grades did the pirate get in school?

High seas.

Why did the failing student apply for a charge card?

He needed extra credit.

I'm a little worried about your being at the bottom of your class.

Don't worry. They teach the same thing at both ends.

I only made three mistakes in
school today.

That's not bad. What were they?
I flunked history, English, and math.

TEACHER: I take real pleasure in giving you a ninety on the test.

PUPIL: Why don't you give me a hundred and really enjoy yourself?

TEACHER (writing on the blackboard): I ain't had no fun all summer. Now how should I correct that?

LITTLE BOY: Get a hobby.

TEACHER: Do you know why you always get such poor marks?

STUDENT: I don't know.

TEACHER: That's right.

What did the horse get on its report cards?

Straight hays.

What's a report card?

A poison-pen letter written by a teacher.

Where do report cards get their education?

In grade school.

TEACHER: Your son has the worst report card I've ever seen.
PARENT: What makes it so bad?
TEACHER: He even flunked recess.

What happened when the sailor saw his report card?

He got "C" sick.

SAILOR: I'm very disappointed in you, son.

SON: Why? I got all A's and B's on my report card.

SAILOR: I was hoping you'd follow in my footsteps and be a "sea" student.

When was the Great Depression?
The last time I got my report card.

MOTHER: Sit down and show me
your report card.
SON: I can't sit down. I just showed
it to Dad.

Why should you never dot another
student's "i"?
*Because you should keep your eyes on
your own paper.*

Why was the computer printer
thrown out of school?
It copied.

How did the babies cheat in nursery school?

They had crib notes.

Why was the little bird punished?

It was caught peeping during a test.

I think I saw you copying off Juan's paper.

No, I didn't.

Okay, what have you got for question eight?

I don't know. He hasn't gotten to that one yet.

Why was the pony suspended from school?

For horsing around.

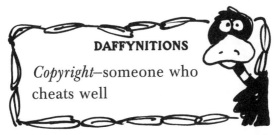

DAFFYNITIONS

Copyright—someone who cheats well

Why did the cow quit school?
She had a beef with the teacher.

Why was the dropout asked to leave
the elegant party?
He had no class.

Why did the left-handed student fail his essay test?

He couldn't right.

Jimmy, how come you're such a perfect idiot?

I spend a lot of time watching you.

TEACHER: If you don't study I may have to put a dunce cap on you.

STUDENT: No, you don't. I can put it on myself.

Where do bellydancers get their education?

At the Navel Academy.

Where did the gangplank get its education?
At boarding school.

Where do cows get their education?
Second dairy school.

Where did the door get its education?
The school of hard knocks.

Where do you learn proper English?
Grammar school.

Is it better to do your homework on a full or empty stomach?
It's better to do it on paper.

Why did the girl get an "incomplete" in her Italian class?
She never turned in her Rome work.

What do pigs do after school?
Their hamwork.

Why do teachers give homework?
*So students will have something to do
when they're not watching TV.*

MIKE: My folks are sending me away to school.

IKE: Why is that?

MIKE: So they won't have to help me with my homework.

HORACE: Mom, the teacher kept me in for something I didn't do.

MORRIS: Really, what was it?

HORACE: My homework.

SON: Dad, could you help with my homework?

FATHER: No. It wouldn't be right.

SON: Well, at least you could try.

FATHER: Our son wants me to help him with his homework.

MOTHER: So, help him while you can, dear. Next year he goes into the fifth grade.

In what subject do insects get their best grades?

A-gnat-omy.

Why did the baby go to chemistry class?

To learn formulas.

What were your two best subjects in nursery school?

Sandbox and resting.

What course teaches you about soda?

Fizz-eology.

Why did the student throw Alka Seltzer into the swimming pool?
So he could study fizz ed.

Why do textbooks carry beepers?
So they can get paged.

What course talks about hamburgers?
Meat-eorology.

What kind of schoolbook does a
tree have?
Looseleaf.

What did the builder write his book
report on?
Construction paper.

TOM SWIFTIES

"I don't want to read *Moby
Dick,*" Tom wailed.

What do porcupines write their
reports with?
Quill pens.

What do insects use to write reports?
Flypaper.

54

MICHAEL: May I borrow your book, *How to Become a Millionaire?*

MICHELE: Sure. Here it is.

MICHAEL: Thanks, but half the book is missing.

MICHELE: What's the matter? Isn't half a million good enough for you?

TEACHER: Why are your writing on a piece of sandpaper?

ASHLEY: You told us to write a rough draft.

What are the most confusing kind of books at the library?

Books of short tall stories.

Why did you go fishing instead of writing your book report?

Book report? I thought you said "brook report"!

Why was the school library so small?
Too many short stories.

LIBRARIAN: We just discovered an overdue library book you've had for some time now.

STUDENT: Do I owe a big fine?

LIBRARIAN: We're naming the new wing after you.

What did the detective say when he arrested the librarian?

"Book 'em!"

BOOK NEVER WRITTEN

Writing a Book Report,
by Phillip D. Paige

What happened when the wheel was invented?

It started a revolution.

What's a pronoun?

A noun that gets paid.

Why did the caterpillar go to the library?
It wanted to become a bookworm.

What is the longest day in the Bible?
The day with no Eve.

What happened when the steam hammer was invented?
It made a big hit.

When is it correct to say, "I is"?
When the teacher asks, "What is the letter after 'H'?"

What punctuation mark is the longest?

The hundred-yard dash.

Why did the fish miss the English class?

It got hooked on phonics.

What's the hardest part of grammar for criminals?

The prison sentence.

You should not say, "I ain't going." You should say, "I'm not going, he's not going, they're not going."

Gee, ain't anybody going?

Why did the spirit study English?
To become a ghostwriter.

TEACHER: "You" is a pronoun.
PUPIL: You is?

What happened when the writing class got hungry?

They ate their words.

Rodney, did you write that poem all by yourself?

Yes, I did.

Then I'm glad to meet you, Mr. Keats. I thought you died 100 years ago.

How is a drama teacher like the Pony Express?

Because he is a stage coach.

I was a hit in the school play. I had the audience glued to their seats.

Wonderful! How clever of you to think of that.

Why did the drama club break their legs?

So they could have a cast party.

Why did the drama club stop functioning?

They couldn't get their act together.

Why was the drama club put in detention?

They kept acting up.

Why did the pool player ruin the school play?

He missed his cue.

HOME RUMORS

Who teaches students to play the flute?

Private tooters.

I got two medals in music. One gold and one silver. The silver one was for playing the piano.

I know, the gold one was for stopping.

Why was the music teacher accused of cruelty?
She beat the drums.

SINGER: I'm thinking of having my ears pierced.
MUSIC TEACHER: You might as well. You pierced mine a long time ago.

What punctuation mark is used in writing dance music?

The polka dot.

What did the brilliant art student make with his brush?

A stroke of genius.

68

What do art teachers do on vacation?
They paint the town red.

Why did the art teacher take her paints to the track meet?
Because the colors ran.

What did the fish do in music class?
Play the scales.

WARPED WISE MAN
Did you hear about the student who got a D minor on his band report card?

69

Why did the art teacher paint the alphabet crimson?

He wanted it to be a red-letter day.

Why did the art student study math?

So she could paint by number.

What do you call a great phys ed
teacher?

A gym dandy.

Why did the locomotive go to the gym?

To join the track team.

What marks did you get in phys ed?

I didn't get marks, only bruises.

BOOK NEVER WRITTEN

Physical Education, by Jim Shorts

Did you get hurt when you were on the football team?

No, only when the team was on me.

STUDENT: The doctor says I can't play football.

COACH: I could have told you that.

COACH: Remember, football develops character, individuality, and leadership.

PLAYER: Yes, coach.

COACH: Now, go out there and do exactly what I tell you.

Why did the crazy gymnast stay on the beam?

He was unbalanced.

TOM SWIFTIES

"She's very good at gymnastics," said Tom flippantly.

74

Why did the football player carry a spare pencil?

In case they needed an extra point.

Why did the tiny ghost join the football team?

He heard they needed a little school spirit.

What did the football coach take with him on his fishing trip?

His tackle.

What do history teachers talk to each other about?

Old times, of course.

LARRY: I wish I had lived a
thousand years ago.
GARY: Why?
LARRY: Because I wouldn't have so
much history to learn.

Can you tell the class the nationality of Napoleon?

Course I can.

That's right.

If George Washington were alive today, what would he be famous for?

Old age.

TEACHER: Can you tell me what happened in 1776?

STUDENT: I can't even tell you what happened last night.

Where do you do arithmetic?

On multiplication tables.

How do you recognize math plants?
They have square roots.

When do math teachers die?
When their number is up.

The president's wife is the first lady.
I thought Eve was.

What's an American president's occupation?
Cabinetmaker.

TEACHER: Now, in history we have had the Stone Age and the Bronze Age. Can anyone name another Age?
SUZIE: The sausage.

Mom, could you help me find the lowest common denominator in this problem?

Don't tell me they haven't found it yet. They were looking for it when I was a child.

How does a young ghost count?
One, boo, three.

What's the best looking geometric
figure?
Acute triangle.

My dog knows math.
He does?
Yes, when I ask him what 10
minus 10 is, he says nothing.

Why did the science teacher and
her husband get divorced?
They didn't have the right chemistry.

Why was the astronomy teacher dizzy?
  She kept seeing stars.

What did the loser at the solar
system competition receive?
  The constellation prize.

TEACHER: What is the formula for water?

ROSE: HIJKLMNO.

TEACHER: Who told you that?

ROSE: You did, you said it was from H to O.

What's the most educated scientific instrument?
A thermometer, because it has so many degrees.

What did the leopard say to his friends in the school cafeteria?
"Save me a spot."

What did the basketball player eat
in the school cafeteria?
   Hoop du jour.

Why was the cafeteria fueled by lamps?
   They were serving a light lunch.

What happened to the vegetables misbehaving in the cafeteria?

They found themselves in hot water.

Notice in school cafeteria: "Shoes are required to eat in the school cafeteria." Someone wrote below the notice: "Socks can eat wherever they want."

Why do cafeteria workers wear roller blades?

So they can serve fast food.

Why did the cafeteria worker want
to become a detective?
So she could grill the hot dogs.

Where is milk stored?
In a cow.

What kind of reviews did the cooking class get?

They were panned.

STUDENT (in the lunchroom, to another student): Will you watch my seat?

OTHER STUDENT: Sure, what time will it be on TV?

JOE: What is sticky, purple, has sixteen legs, and is covered with hair?

MOE: I don't know.

JOE: Neither do I, but they're serving it in the school cafeteria.

Who is in charge of school supplies?
The ruler.

How was the cooking class performance?
Well done.

Why did the English student stuff a handkerchief in his mouth?
So he could become a gag writer.

ANDY: My sister ate some bad chicken in the school cafeteria yesterday.
SANDY: Croquette?
ANDY: Not yet, but she's awfully sick.

How did the school custodian make all his money?
He really cleaned up at work.

What happened when the school custodian ran for election?
He was swept into office.

What club do fish like to join?
The debating team.

Why did the banana become a cheerleader?

So it could do banana splits.

Why did the school camera club close?

It lost its focus.

Why did the exterminator go to the camera club?

It was full of shutterbugs.

What group do happy students join?

The glee club.

Why did the bear join the school paper?

It wanted to be a cub reporter.

Why was the school newspaper delivered to the submarine?

It had a subscription.

Why did the cat take a computer course?

To get hold of a mouse.

TOM SWIFTIES

"I work on the school newspaper," Tom reported.

Knock, knock.
  Who's there?

Oblong.
  Oblong who?

Oblong to the computer club.

94

Why did the computer go to the school cafeteria?

It wanted a few bytes.

What snack did the computer laptop have?

Computer chips.

CRAZY CLASSMATES

MOM: Joey brought a note from school.

DAD: What did it say?

MOM: They want a written excuse for his presence.

A class has a top and bottom. What is in the middle?

The student body.

How should you e-mail a student?

First class.

Why were the students able to study underwater?

Because they had a sub.

Who was the most feared student in the Old West?

Bully the Kid.

IN TRANSYLVANIA, WE LEARN TO *COUNT*!!

FATHER: What did you learn in school today?

SON: I learned to say "Yes, sir," "No, sir," and "Thank you."

FATHER: You did?

SON: Yup.

MOTHER: Why are you home so early?

DAUGHER: The teacher asked me how far I could count and I counted all the way home.

SON: Dad, the teacher thinks I should have a hard drive.

DAD: Hard drive, my eye. You can walk to school just like I did.

SCHOOL NURSE: I think you should take something for that cold.

PUPIL: Oh, good. I'll take the week off.

DRIVING Class

Why was the driver's ed teacher
fired?
He couldn't get it into gear.

Why did the vowels take driver's ed?
So they could make a U turn.

Why was the classroom so crowded?
  It was the class of 2000.

How can you leave a classroom with
two legs and come back with six?
  Bring a chair back with you.

How is an empty classroom like a
teacher with her eyes closed?
  Because there are no pupils to be seen.

Why did the girl refuse to stand in
line to get to the auditorium?
  *She didn't want to be on an assembly
  line.*

What do cows do best in driver's ed?
 Steer.

How did the driver's ed class
celebrate getting new tires?
 With a real blowout.

102

TEACHER (to young man running in the hall): I'm going to have to report you to the principal. What's your name?

STUDENT: Ignatius Cornelius Fagenheimer.

TEACHER: Well, don't let me catch you doing it again.

Why don't schools cheat?
They have principals.

WARPED WISE MAN
Old principals never die. They just lose their faculties.

Where do sheep go after high school?
The ewe-niversity.

Who always fires the cannon at
military school?
Some big shot.

PRINCIPAL: This is the fifth time this week you've been in my office. What do you have to say for yourself?
STUDENT: I'm glad it's Friday.

Why should you never mention the number 288 in front of the school principal?
Because it is too gross.

Would you like to go to Heaven?
Yes, but my mother told me to come home right after Sunday school.

Why did you have to stay after school?

The teacher asked me to write a paper on laziness and I turned in a blank piece of paper.

TEACHER: Now be sure and go
straight home after school.
PUPIL: I can't, Teacher.
TEACHER: Why not?
PUPIL: I live around the corner.

Knock-knock.
Who's there?
Stain.
Stain who?
Stain late after school.

BOOK NEVER WRITTEN
After School, by Dee Tension

Why do old schoolteachers never die?
They just grade away.

When is a teacher like a bird of
prey?
When she watches you like a hawk.

What's the difference between a train conductor and a teacher?
One minds the train and the other trains the mind.

Why did the schoolteacher excuse the firefly?
Because if you have to glow, you have to glow.

Why are teachers rather special?
They are usually in a class by themselves.

FIRE DRILL!

JERRY: I don't think my teacher likes me.

TERRY: Why do you say that?

JERRY: During fire drills he tells me to stay in my seat.

110

SALLY: My teacher doesn't even
  know what a horse looks like.
MOM: That's impossible.
SALLY: Well, I drew a picture of a
  horse and she asked me what it
  was.

As a teacher, do you think my
daughter is trying?
  Yes, your daughter is the most
trying student in class.

TEACHER: Who knows the story
  "Once upon a time…"?
PUPIL: I know that one.
TEACHER: Okay, how does it end?
STUDENT: "Happily ever after."

What kind of invention was the
clock?

A timely one.

What state has no capital?

A state of mind.

Why is a boat the cheapest form of transportation?

It runs on water.

STUDENT: What good is the rain, Teacher?

TEACHER: It makes things grow—the grass, the flowers, the trees.

STUDENT: Then why does it rain on the sidewalk?

PUPIL: What is "extinct"?

TEACHER: Well, if all life on earth were wiped out, you could say the human race was extinct.

PUPIL: But who would you say it to?

If it takes five men fifteen hours to build a brick wall, how long would it take ten men to do it?

Why should they do it at all? The five men just did it.

What was the highest mountain
before Mt. Everest was discovered?
Mt. Everest, of course.

How can you tell when a swimming
team is broke?
It can't keep its head above water.

What did the swimming coach do in
the boxing match?
He took a dive.

Why did they stop playing water
polo at school?
All the horses kept drowning.

Where's the fencing coach?
Out to lunge.

How did they know the swimming
team was inexperienced?
They were all wet behind the ears.

116

Father (talking to his son who marched in the school band during half-time at the football game): "I'm proud of you, Son. Everyone else in the band was marching out of step but you."

RUNNER: How did I do, coach? Did you take my time?
COACH: I didn't have to. You took it yourself.

TOM SWIFTIES

"I scored a goal," said Tom, making a point.

Why is a geometry teacher so boring?
Because he's a square and talks in circles.

Why is 3 + 3 = 7 like our left foot?
Because it isn't right.

118

What's the best way to pass a geometry test?

Know all the angles.

I wish you would pay a little attention to your math.

Well, I do. I pay as little attention as possible.

That last joke was like a math problem—hard to figure out.

Why does a math teacher have his head in the clouds?

Because he offers pi in the sky.

TEACHER: If you had three apples
and ate one, what would you have?

JEFF: Three.

TEACHER: Three?

JEFF: Yes, two on the outside and
one on the inside.

120

TEACHER: How much is 5 plus 5?
MIKE: Ten.
TEACHER: Very good.
MIKE: Very good? It's perfect.

What does a hungry math teacher like to eat best?
A square meal.

What happened when the chemistry students met?
It was lab at first sight.

What's a geology teacher's favorite movie?
"Rocky."

Who was the first couple to study science?

Atom and Eve.

What mouthwash do bio teachers use?

Micro-scope.

What's the most important thing
about the 18th-century scientists?
They are all dead.

PROFESSOR: Everyone knows that
Alexander Graham Bell invented
the telephone. What did his
assistant Mr. Watson do?
SILLY STUDENT: He sent out the
phone bills.

AL: What did the dinosaurs eat?
MAL: Judging from the ones I saw in
the museum, they didn't eat
anything.

What happens when vowels lend money?

They end up with an IOU.

What's the connecting link between the animal and vegetable kingdoms?

Stew.

TEACHER: Please use the following word in a sentence: "districts."

STUDENT: Okay. "Districts the best anyone has done since Houdini."

TEACHER: Now use "flounder."

STUDENT: All right. "I looked for my sister and flounder in the library."

TEACHER: Can you use "decide"?

STUDENT: Sure. "The truck driver parked on decide of the road."

TEACHER: Now, "odyssey."

STUDENT: "You odyssey the movie I told you about."

126

TEACHER: How about "pursuit"?

STUDENT: Be glad to. "The store clerk said the price was $100 pursuit."

TEACHER: Try "boycott."

STUDENT: How's this? "The boycott his pants on the fence."

What happened when the English teacher's dictionary was stolen?

She was at a loss for words.

What day of school is the children's favorite?

The last.

TEACHER: Are you paying attention?

STUDENT: Yes, teacher.

TEACHER: Then why is your nose buried in that comic book?

STUDENT: I'm paying attention to the comic book.

What do you call someone who sleeps in class?

Bored of education.

What do you call a school where all the students are over six feet tall?

A high school.

What kind of boats are designed for students?

Scholarships.

What do you call a pupil who sneezes in class?

A wheeze kid.

What is your name?

Charles.

Charles what?

Oh, that's okay. Just call me
Charles.

TEACHER: Your behavior is terrible. How many more times will I have to tell you about it?

LES: 47.

TEACHER: 47?

LES: Yes, that's the number of days before summer vacation.

HISTORY'S MYSTERIES

What do you get when you cross the alphabet with the tennis team?

Love letters.

Why did the mailman take the alphabet?
So he could deliver the letters.

Why was the alphabet tired out?
It was spellbound.

What do you get when you cross the English department with the school cafeteria?
Alphabet soup.

How does a blackboard handle bad times?
It chalks them up to experience.

TEACH: What does N-E-W spell?
STU: New.
TEACH: And what does K-N-E-W spell?
STU: Canoe.

That last joke made as much sense as an open-book spelling test.

MOM: Who are you writing to?

SUE: Myself.

MOM: What does the letter say?

SUE: I don't know. I haven't received it yet.

What's the best way to cut down on air pollution in schools?

Use unleaded pencils.

What did the ruler say to the pencil?

"You have to draw the line somewhere."

Why did the pencil sharpener keep arguing with the pencil?

The sharpener was trying to make a point.

RICKY: What do you wanna do?
DICKIE: I've got an idea. Let's flip a
coin. Heads we go fishing and
tails we go biking. If it lands on
its side we go home and study.

136

FATHER: Hard work never killed anyone.

SON: That's the trouble. I want to engage in something that has a little danger to it.

TEACHER (to new class): When I call on you I'd like you to stand up and tell everyone your name.

FIRST BOY: My name is Julie.

TEACHER: Please tell us your full name. Your name is Julius. Okay, next. What is your name?

SECOND BOY: I guess my name is Billius.

Why did the electrician go to school?

To study current events.

Do you go to school stupid?
Yes, and I come out the same way.

Knock, knock.
Who's there?
Don Juan.
Don Juan who?
Don Juan to go to school today.

Why did the optometrist go to school?
To keep an eye on things.

Why did the student come to school with two clocks?
He wanted to keep up with the times.

When fish swim in schools, who helps their teacher?
The herring aid.

Why did the cabbie rush to school?
To take a crash course.

How did the hairstylist feel about school?

Shear delight.

What does a sick teacher take?

Pu-pils.

Why did the teacher try to return her pupils?

They were exchange students.

What did the teacher say to the naughty hornet?

"Beehive yourself."

TEACHER: Thank you for giving me
an apple. But tell me, why did
you give me only the core?
JOAN: Do you like apples?
TEACHER: Yes, I do.
JOAN: So do I.

MOTHER: What do you want for your birthday, dear?

LITTLE MARY: A trip to the moon.

MOTHER: But you're too young to go.

LITTLE MARY: Then send my teacher.

TEACHER: "The early bird catches the worm." What does that mean?

STUDENT: Some animals don't care what they eat.

GIRL: My teacher talks to herself all the time.

BOY: So does mine, but she thinks that we're listening.

PROF: This test is multiple choice.
STU: Then I choose not to take it.

How does a lobster remember the answers to a test?

By tying a string around his claw.

How did the wrestler pin down the answers to the test?

He put a hold on them.

Why didn't the dry cleaner finish the test?

He had pressing problems.

This exam will be conducted on the honor system. Please take a seat apart and in alternate rows.

FIRST STUDENT: Did you pass the test on the North Pole?
SECOND STUDENT: I knew it cold.

MOTHER: Your grades are terrible. You have C's and D's on your report card.

CHILD: Those aren't grades. They're vitamin deficiencies.

How did the duck do on its report card?

All its grades were down.

FATHER: Son, I want you to have all the things I didn't have.

SON: You mean like all A's on your report card?

TOM SWIFTIES

"There's an exam today," said Tom testily.

"But I'm all for exams," Tom protested.

What can you never make with
shaky penmanship?
Straight A's.

TED: The driver in front of us must be one of my teachers.

DAD: Why do you say that?

TED: He's so stubborn about letting us pass.

TEACHER: Do you know why you get such poor grades?

BETTY: I don't know.

TEACHER: Exactly.

TOM SWIFTIES

"Sure, I'm grading your paper again," Tom's teacher remarked.

"I might get a better grade if I gave the teacher an apple," said Tom fruitlessly.

TV STAR: Son, let me see your
report card. I hope you did well
in the ratings.

SON: I sure did. In fact my school
wants me to sign up to do another
13 weeks this summer.

TEACHER: Tommy, why haven't you brought back your report card?

TOMMY: It's because of the two A's you gave me. My parents are showing it to all my relatives.

SON: Here's my report card, Dad, along with one of your old ones that I found in the attic. As you see they're almost identical.

DAD: You're right, Son. I guess the only fair thing is to give you the same thing my dad gave to me.

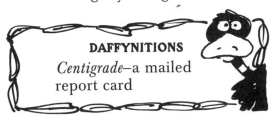

DAFFYNITIONS

Centigrade–a mailed report card

Why was the steer suspended from school?

He was the class bully.

TEACHER: Where is the Red Sea?
PEE WEE: On my report card.

Why did the robin flunk out of school?

He was a bird brain.

Why did the fashion-conscious student fail?

She had a clothes mind.

Why did the student carry a parachute to school?

He was planning to drop out.

Where do travel agents learn their trade?

Vacational school.

Do you like homework?
I like nothing better.

Where do mothers learn to feed
their babies?
Nursery school.

Where do compasses get their education?

West Point.

Where do furniture polishers get their education?

At finishing school.

TEACHER: Jose, did you do your homework?

JOSE: No, I thought you covered the subject pretty well in class.

What kind of homework do trolls bring home from school?

Gnomework.

What course teaches you about raw fish?

Sushi-ology.

What course do yodelers take?

Echo-nomics.

What's a cat's best subject?
  Meow-sic.

What's a parrot's favorite?
  Polly-tics.

TEACHER: Why didn't you do your homework?
STUDENT: The hard drive ate it.

DAFFYNITIONS

Writer's cramp—what you develop when it's time to do your homework

Homework—schoolwork to go

What do you call books read by
Dallas students?
Tex books.

Why did the tree pick up a book?
To leaf through it.

158

Where do sleepy students carry their books?

In a napsack.

Why did the high school senior tie himself up?

So he'd be bound for college.

Why did the student beat up his texts?

He was told to hit the books.

Why was the library so crowded?

It was booked up.

What's a pig's skin used for?
To keep the pig together.

What would you get if you crossed
the school library with a genius?
A novel idea.

How do you grade libraries?
With bookmarks.

Who guards the school library?
The bookkeeper.

Can you name the capital of every
state in America in 10 seconds?
Washington, D.C.

Why shouldn't you pollute the ocean?
Because it makes the sea sick.

What is the leading cause of dry skin?
Towels.

JEST
TESTING

Why did the word processor fall in
love with the English teacher?
  She was his type.

Why did everyone think the English teacher was very old?

She said she taught Shakespeare.

Why did the plywood join the debating team?

So it could have a panel discussion.

TEACHER: Nobody ever heard a sentence without a predicate.

WISE WILLY: I have: "Thirty days."

What's the difference between an active verb and a passive verb?

An active verb shows action and a passive verb shows passion.

ENGLISH TEACHER: Robert Burns
    wrote "To a Field Mouse."
PUPIL: I'll bet he didn't get an answer.

Who replaced the music teacher?
    The substi-toot.

TEACHER: Today we will discuss *The Hunchback of Notre Dame*. Who can tell us about Quasimodo? Michael, can you?

MICHAEL: No, but the name does ring a bell.

Why were the music students allowed to roam the halls?

They had notes from their teacher.

TOM SWIFTIES

"Poetry is not one of my favorite subjects," Tom said adversely.

HALA-BOO-YA!

What do ghosts sing in the glee club?
  Spirituals.

Where did the rhino sit in the
school band?
  The horn section.

MUSIC TEACHER: Dream you are a lark singing in the meadow.

STUDENT: I'd rather dream I was an elephant and squirt water through my nose.

Why did they say the school band was unsinkable?
Nobody could drown them out.

A unicorn has one horn and a bull has two. Does anything have more?
Yes, an orchestra.

MUSIC STUDENT: Do you think I'll ever be able to do something with my voice?

MUSIC TEACHER: It might come in handy in case of a fire.

Why did the donut join the basketball team?

To practice dunking.

What happened when the basketball team brought razors to the game?

They were accused of shaving points.

What happened when the lollipops played against the school team?

They got licked.

TOM SWIFTIES

"Music is my worst subject," Tom noted flatly.

BASKETBALL COACH: I believe you've grown two feet over the summer.

PLAYER: No, coach. I still have only two.

What team cries when it loses?

The bawl team.

What did George Washington's father say when he saw his report card?

"George, you're going down in history."

Why did the history book go out so much?

It had a lot of dates.

What does a banana need to become president?

A peel.

TEACHER: Columbus discovered America over 400 years ago.
STUDENT: Gee, what a memory you've got.

Where are you going in such a hurry?

I just bought a new history book and I'm trying to get to class before it gets out of date.

Who came after our 35th president?
The 36th president.

TEACHER: At your age I could name all the presidents and in the right order.

SMART ALEX: Sure, but at that time there were only five of them.

Why did the baker go to math class?
To learn the value of pi.

What type of math do sharpshooters
study?
Trigger-nometry.

TEACHER: In this country everyone can become president. Everyone has a chance.

YOUNG BOY: I'll sell mine for five dollars.

If 12 make a dozen, how many make a billion?

Very few.

Why did the carpenter study math?

So he could build multiplication tables.

Why couldn't the ruler stand up in class?

It only had one foot.

Do you like arithmetic?

Sum of it.

Is a hammer a useful tool in math?
No, but multi-pliers are.

Why did they call the geology
teacher crazy?
He had rocks in his head.

What did the science teacher get
when she cloned a piece of coal?
A carbon copy.

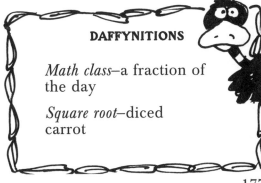

DAFFYNITIONS

Math class–a fraction of
the day

Square root–diced
carrot

What do fashionable biology
students wear?
Designer genes.

Name the constituents of quartz.
Pints.

What do earth science students
weigh themselves on?
The Richter scale.

A geologist thinks nothing of ten
   thousand years.
Oh, no! I lent a geologist ten dollars
   yesterday.

How was your geology lecture?
I was rocked to sleep.

TOM SWIFTIES

"The sun emits ultraviolet rays,"
said Tom, shedding some light
on the science class discussion.

Who studies on the highway?
Road scholars.

When water becomes ice, what is
the greatest change?
The price.

Our subject today is overcrowding.
Who can give me an example of
overcrowding?
Rub-a-dub-dub, three men in a
tub.

What do you call a place where a
law student lives?
A legal pad.

YELLOW JACKET: Are you good in
    school?
WASP: Yes, I'm a bee student.

Why was the little schoolhouse red?
They ran out of green paint.

182

What happened to the student who swallowed the dictionary?

The nurse couldn't get a word out of him.

Could you forgive a bully who insulted or hit you?

I think I could, especially if he was bigger than me.

How old is your grandmother?

I don't know, but we've had her for quite a while.

What's the most educated room in the house?

The study.

How did the mummy react to the dull class?

It was bored stiff.

MOE: What happened to you?

JOE: I just had a run-in with the school bully.

MOE: How did it happen?

JOE: He said he had half a mind to beat me up.

MOE: And you agreed to let him beat you up?

JOE: No, I agreed he had half a mind.

What course do golfers take?

Driver's ed.

Why was the driver's ed teacher so lucky?
He had all the brakes.

How was the driving teacher's parking?
It was unparalleled.

How did Darth Vader's parents get him to study?

By using the Force.

Why did the computer screen go to school?

So it could become a school monitor.

Why did the baby computer stay away from school?

It had a bad virus.

What did the pig put in the school computer?

Sloppy disks.

PRINCIPAL: Good job, Robert. Your essay, "Why Video Games are a Waste of Time," won the $50 grand prize.

ROBERT: Gee, that's great! Could I have it all in quarters?

188

PRINCIPAL: What's your name,
   young man?
BOY: Paul.
PRINCIPAL: Say "sir".
BOY: All right, Sir Paul.

TEACHER: Please use this word in a
   sentence: "centimeter."
STUDENT: Sure. "My sister was
   walking home from school, so I
   was centimeter."

Why did the vampire want to go to
the biology class?
   He heard the teacher was an old bat.

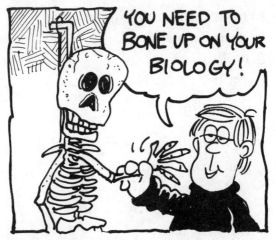

What do skeletons call study
periods?
Skull sessions.

Who teaches goats at home?
Their nanny.

How did the teacher handle a class full of baby goats?

With kid gloves.

What did the teacher say to the plumber taking classes?

"Pipe down."

TEACHER: What did you do this weekend?

STUDENT: Johnny and me went to the ballgame.

TEACHER: Johnny and I.

STUDENT: No, you weren't there.

What's the first thing to do with a barrel of crude oil?

Teach it some manners.

Where does it never rain?

Under an umbrella.

Everyone says we should conserve energy. How can we do that?
By staying in bed all day.

GIRL MONSTER: Mommy, Teacher said I was neat, pretty, and well-behaved.
MOMMY MONSTER: Don't worry, dear. You'll do better next time.

SILLY: I know someone 30 years old who's still in the fifth grade.
SALLY: No way!
SILLY: Yeah, she's my teacher.

When does a track star put a faucet
on his leg?
When he has water on the knee.

Why was the math teacher fired?
He went off on a tangent.

Why did the track star enter the
student government?
So he could run for office.

What would you get if you crossed
an English teacher with the track
team?
A run-on sentence.

Why did the camera club go to the
track meet?
They were hoping for a photo finish.

Why did the supermodel get an "A" in math?

She was great with figures.

Why do geometric figures never meet?

They travel in different circles.

Why is Noah called the father of the circle?

He made the first arc.

If you had ten lemons and I offered you seven, what would you have?

Ten. I don't like lemons.

What would you have if you had five apples in one hand and three in the other?

Huge hands.

Who do you think is responsible for the high cost of electricity?

The man who comes to read the meter.

TEACHER'S PESTS

Who did the science teacher give
his Bunsen burner to?
  His old flame.

Why did the astronomy teacher search through the school cafeteria utensils?

He was looking for the big dipper.

What job did the skull apply for in science?

Department head.

Did you know that oxygen was discovered in 1774?

What did people breathe before that?

What would happen if there were no water on earth?

We'd all be thirsty.

TEACHER (trying to teach the pupils about magnets): This morning we are going to discuss something that starts with the letter "M". It has six letters and picks up things. What is it?

SMART ALEX: I know. "Mother."

Why don't geometry teachers like modern music?

Because they are squares.

What would you get if you crossed the geology department with the school band?

Rock music.

What did the skeleton play in the school band?

The trom-bone.

Why couldn't the music teacher get into the classroom?

All the keys were in the piano.

How do law students date?
They court each other.

What piece of underwear did the
law student carry in his attache case?
His briefs.

TEACHER: Please use the following word in a sentence: "acquire."

PUPIL: All right. The girl loved to sing so she joined acquire.

MOTHER: I'm worried about you getting enough sleep.

DAUGHTER: Aw, Mom, don't worry. I make up for lost sleep in class.

DAD: Look at those kids all riding to school! When I was young we walked 10 miles to get to school.

SON: Did you like school?

DAD: I sure did.

SON: What was your favorite subject?

DAD: Walking.

What college do vines go to?
The Ivy League.

What college do lovers go to?
Embraceable U.

TEACHER: Have you been fighting again? I told you to count to 100 before doing anything when you're angry.

SAMMY: Yes, but the other boy's teacher told him to count to 50.

Knock, knock.
Who's there?

School.
School who?

School as a cucumber.

Why did the student glue himself to his report?
He was trying to stick to the subject.

PARENT: I want to take my son out of this lousy college.

DEAN: But, sir, he's at the head of this college.

PARENT: That's how I know it's a lousy college.

206

Why did the thermometer go to college?

To pick up a few degrees.

Why were the walls of the university covered with ivy?

Because they couldn't afford paint.

ED: My uncle is in medical school.
NED: What's he studying?
ED: Nothing, they're studying him.

You tell me your son is a well-known writer, but he's only in college. Does he write for money?

Yes, in every letter.

...THE INSTRUCTIONS ARE *ELF-EXPLANATORY*

TEST

What do elves learn in school?
The elf-abet.

What would you get if you crossed
the alphabet with a shackle?
A chain letter.

How do you say goodbye to the alphabet?

"A B C'ing you."

Why did the little girl watch the alphabet?

She was told to mind her P's and Q's.

TEACHER: What does "L-O-W" spell?

STUDENT: Low.

TEACHER: And if I put a "B" in front of it? What now?

STUDENT: Below.

TEACHER: Please spell "Tennessee."

STUDENT: One-a-see, two-a-see....

Why did the farmer go to school?
*He heard they were having a field
trip.*

Why did the speed demon go to class?
To take an accelerated course.

What school event do labor leaders like?

Re-unions.

What did the billboard learn at school?

Sign language.

What did the Parisian teacher make when she raised her glass?

A French toast.

Why didn't the teacher believe the little ghost's excuse?

She could see right through it.

What did the turtles say to the teacher?

"You tortoise everything we know."

Why did the teacher's watch go "tick, tick, tick"?

It wasn't allowed to tock in class.

RICKY: This new watch I got is waterproof and can tell time underwater.

ROCKY: That's nothing. I dropped my watch into the Mississippi River three years ago and it's still running.

RICKY: The same watch?

ROCKY: Nope, the Mississippi.

Before we start the final exam, are there any questions?

Yes, what's the name of this course?

TEACHER: Remember the story of the lamb who strayed from the flock and was eaten by the wolf. If he had remained with the flock, he wouldn't have been eaten by the wolf, would he?

PUPIL: No, ma'am. He would have been eaten by us.

214

TEACHER: I'm having trouble with one of my students.

PRINCIPAL: What's wrong?

TEACHER: Not only is he the worst-behaved child in class, he also has a perfect attendance record.

TEACHER: You got excused because you said your grandma was dying. Today I saw her in the beauty parlor.

STUDENT: She was dyeing her hair. Now she's a blonde.

TEACHER: I thought you promised me you'd pass the test.

STUDENT: I did. I passed it on to the kid behind me.

CINDY: Mommy, Mommy, I made a
90 on my test paper.
MOM: Great. Did anyone make 100?
CINDY: Yes. All the other kids.

Why was the jump rope thrown out
of school?

It kept skipping classes.

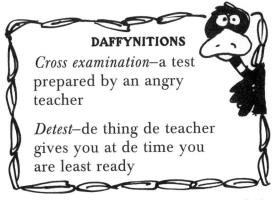

DAFFYNITIONS

Cross examination—a test
prepared by an angry
teacher

Detest—de thing de teacher
gives you at de time you
are least ready

What do you call Oreos that skip class?

Cookie cutters.

What's a magician's favorite subject?

Trick-enometry.

Why were the poorer students removed from school?
They were outclassed.

Why did the failing student feel ashamed?
He was degraded.

What do you call a cartoon that's been put out of school?
Suspended animation.

Where did the ornamental bracelet get its education?
Charm school.

Where did King Arthur send his court?

Knight school.

Where does a dwarf go to school?

An institute of lower learning.

220

Where do politicians learn to be candidates?
Primary school.

What's a spendthrift's favorite subject?
Shop.

Why did the student bring his wallet to speech class?
He heard that money talks.

BOOK NEVER WRITTEN

How to Finish Homework on Time,
by Willy B. Dunn

Where do you go to take a course in
making ice cream?
Sundae school.

Who only reads underground?
Bookworms.

What did the carpenter make for the textbook?

A table of contents.

What did the Civil War book say when it left?

"I'm history."

What do you get when you cross a goat with a kangaroo?

A kid with a built-in school bag.

How do you define "buoyant"?

A male insect.

What is it that we find so easy to get into and so hard to get out of?
Bed.

Which month has 28 days?
They all do.

What do you get when you cross a class clown with Mr. Spock?

A funny Vulcan.

TEACHER: Can you describe an elevator?

STUDENT: Sure, it's a small room you go into and when you shut the door, the upstairs comes down.

TEACHER: Now, can you tell me something that is dangerous to get close to and has a horn?

STUDENT: A car.

SQUARE ONE

TEACHER: Can you use the word "descent" in a sentence?

STUDENT: Sure. "The dog followed descent to catch the robber."

TEACHER: How about the word "terrain"?

STUDENT: Okay. "I saw the weather channel and it's supposed terrain tonight."

TEACHER: Now, how about the word "hatchet"?

STUDENT: Be glad to. "The chicken sat on the egg to hatchet."

FATHER: When Lincoln was your age he walked 10 miles to go to school.

SON: And when he was your age he was president.

Why did the school orchestra terminate?
It disbanded.

MOTHER: What is this 60 in history?
DAUGHTER: I think that's the size of
the class.

HISTORY TEACHER: Mary, can you tell me about Lincoln's Gettysburg Address?

MARY: I can call information and get the phone number.

Why did you skip so many history classes?

I didn't think I'd have to go every day. History repeats itself.

Can you tell me something important that didn't exist years ago?

Yeah, me.

What did the dance teacher call her dancing sibling?

A stepsister.

Why did the glee club members get along so well together?

They were all in a chord.

Why did the piano teacher chase the elephant with a feather?

She wanted to tickle his ivories.

Why was the voice teacher so good at baseball?

She had perfect pitch.

How is the baseball slugger doing in school?

Batter.

Why did the composer coach the baseball team?

Because he knew how to score.

Why did the coach bring the crate to the baseball game?

He wanted to see the box score.

Where do detergents sit in the ballpark?

The bleachers.

What math tool do baseball players use?

A slide rule.

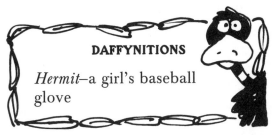

DAFFYNITIONS

Hermit–a girl's baseball glove

Who did the math teacher date?
A real hot number.

How did the student do in fractions?
He wasn't half bad.

What would you get if you crossed the tennis team with geometric figures?

A love triangle.

Why did the student eat geometric figures?

So he could have three square meals a day.

If you cut two apples and three pears into 10 pieces each, what would you have?

Fruit salad.

Why did the jailor buy a
microscope?
He liked to look at the cells.

What kind of jokes did Einstein like?
Wisecracks.

236

FATHER: Son, what did you learn in school today?

SON: In math we learned pi r squared.

FATHER: That's silly. Everyone knows pies are round.

What do astronomy students scrub sinks with?

Comet.

Where does a student talk about his experiments?

The science blab.

SCIENCE TEACHER: Did you know
  that grasshoppers have antennas?
FRED: Oh, do they get cable?

What is meant by Hobson's choice?
  Mrs. Hobson, I guess.

TEACHER: What is more important, the sun or the moon?

CHRISTOPHER: The moon, because it shines when it's dark. The sun shines during the day when it's light anyway.

TEACHER: Alice, your father is a doctor. Can you tell us what an appendectomy is?

ALICE: About $5,000.

Who wears different kinds of clothing all at the same time?

A student body.

...WE'RE PEN PALS!

MOE: I guess my pen will have to go on itching.

FOE: Why?

MOE: Because I ran out of scratch paper.

KAREN: May I leave the room?
TEACHER: Well, you can't take it with you.

FIRST STUDENT: What's the hardest thing for you in school?
SECOND STUDENT: Whispering to the person next to me without moving my lips.

MIKE: I finally finished that jigsaw puzzle.
IKE: Did it take you long?
MIKE: The box said from eight to twelve years, but I finished it in less than a month.

Why did the student wear a leash to school?

He wanted to be teacher's pet.

Why is a school day like a jury trial?

They both end in recesses.

What class tells you about
corridors?
Study hall.

Why was the dried grape called on
in school?
It was raisin its hand.

How many ribs do you have?
I don't know, I'm too ticklish to
count them.

Why was the geography teacher so
popular with her students?
She gave them a lot of latitude.

What did the chicken teach the typing class?
Hunt and peck.

What is an octopus?
An eight-sided cat.

What did the teacher rabbit tell her bunnies?

Hare-raising stories.

Name a great timesaver.

Love at first sight.

TEACHER: I have good news and bad news. The good news is that there will be half a day of school on Monday morning.

JOHNNY: What's the bad news?

TEACHER: The bad news is that there will be another half a day Monday afternoon.

TEACHER: Alan, your handwriting is atrocious.

ALAN: That's all right, I'm going to be a doctor.

That last joke had as much class as an unemployed school teacher.

TEACHER: Henry, what did you do this weekend?

HENRY: I went fishing and caught 20 catfish, each weighing over 10 pounds.

TEACHER: Now, Henry, suppose I tell you a story just as silly. I was trying to get into my car when a gorilla came up to me and tried to attack me. This little dog came and scared the gorilla away. Do you believe that?

HENRY: Of course. That was my dog.

Why did the high-schooler try out
for soccer?
It was his goal in life.

What soccer player is never promoted?
The left back.

Why do so many students join the soccer team?

Just for kicks.

Why is a poor math student like a crossed telephone line?

They both get a lot of wrong numbers.

What kind of geometric shape keeps falling apart?

A wrecktangle.

BOOK NEVER WRITTEN

How to Pass a Final Exam,
by Noah Lott

... I'M FEELING *HALF BAKED!*

TEACHER: If you had four apples and I asked you for two, how many would you have?

MARTY: Four.

TEACHER: Why?

MARTY: Because I wouldn't give you any.

What happens when you fail geometry?

It's back to square one.

Why was the math teacher so self-absorbed?

He was looking out for number one.

If you had 200 pennies, 100 nickels and 75 quarters in your pocket, what would you have?

Droopy pants.

BOOK NEVER WRITTEN
It All Adds Up, by Cal Q. Late

Why did the math teacher join the glee club?

She wanted to sing a few numbers.

How did the corn do in the band?

It played by ear.

252

Why did the soloist turn her back
on the school band?
She didn't want to face the music.

Why did the millionaire give the
music school a new piano?
He was an organ donor.

Why did the guitar leave music class?
Everyone kept picking on it.

TOM SWIFTIES

"I broke my leg and couldn't
come to school last week,"
said Tom lamely.

FIRST CLASSMATE: I'm first in English class!

SECOND CLASSMATE: I'm first in math!

THIRD CLASSMATE: Well, when the bell rings, I'm first out the door.

TEACHER: You're late. Would you please take a seat?
DIM: Sure. Where to?

TEACHER: An anonymous person is one who doesn't wish to be known.
PUPIL: That's a stupid definition.
TEACHER: Why said that?
PUPIL: An anonymous person.

Why didn't the lamb graduate?
It was left baa-ck.

Where do athletes go to college?
The uni-varsity.

What does a dog get when it
graduates from obedience school?
A pedigree.

How can you tell an Ivy League door?
It has a Yale lock.

What do you get when you graduate from the police academy?

The third degree.

What is it called when two students are admitted to college for the price of one?

Two-ition.

MAN: What is your son taking in college?

FATHER: Everything I have.

Father's note to son in college: "Here's the $10 you requested. By the way, $10 is written with one zero, not two."

Why did the absent-minded
professor put glue on his head?
*He thought it would make things stick
in his mind.*

HOSPITAL NURSE (to the absent-minded professor): "It's a boy, sir!"

PROFESSOR: Well, what does he want?

FIRST COLLEGE STUDENT: You look upset. What's wrong?

SECOND STUDENT: I wrote home for money to buy a study lamp.

FIRST STUDENT: So what happened?

SECOND STUDENT: They sent me the lamp.

PROFESSOR: Haven't you a brother who took this course last year?

STUDENT: No, sir. I'm just taking it again.

PROFESSOR: Amazing resemblance.

A professor driving near a university campus saw a student being chased by three dogs. He stopped the car and shouted, "Quick! Get in!"

"Thanks," said the student. "Most people won't give me a lift when they see I have three dogs."

WISE QUACKS

What's the highest quality school class?

First grade.

What education is geared to helping students get jobs?

Hire education.

Why did the third grader bring a lightbulb to school?

He had a bright idea.

What did the lobster give its teacher?

A crab apple.

Why couldn't the tree answer the teacher's question?

It was stumped.

YOU'RE MY BEST STUDENT, DEER!

What do you call it when a teacher promotes a male deer?

Passing the buck.

TEACHER: Sometimes I think no one in this class hears a thing I say.

CAREY: What?

264

TEACHER: Do you think you're the teacher in this class?

BOBBY: No, sir.

TEACHER: Then don't act like a fool.

BOY: Mom, my teacher told me not to take any more baths.

MOM: Are you sure that's what she said?

BOY: Well, she told me to stay out of hot water.

WARPED WISE MAN

A teacher who goes to school early is in a class by herself.

Where do children in Finland
study?
  At Finishing school.

Where did Batman learn?
  Fly-by-night school.

TEACHER: Would you walk to school in the rain, snow, or sleet?
PUPIL: No, never.
TEACHER: Then what would you walk to school in?
PUPIL: My sneakers.

In what school do you have to drop out before you graduate?
Parachute school.

Where did the high-school student's younger brother go to school?
Junior high.

Why did the injured skeleton take up sewing?
So his bones would knit.

What class is full of wise guys?
The freshmen class.

What did the baker get at school?
He made the honor roll.

What did the lobster major in at the police academy?
Claw enforcement.

What do you call the study of seaweed?
Algae-bra.

Many people think fish is brain food.

I don't think so. If they're so smart, why do so many of them get caught?

If "can't" is short for "cannot", what is "don't" short for?

Doughnut.

Now a problem in arithmetic. If your family owed $30 to the phone company, $250 to the landlord and $50 for utilities, what would they have to pay?

Nothing–we'd move to another town.

What was Samuel Clemens's pen name?

He never had a name for his pen.

Why did the diaper quit the
wrestling team?
It was always getting pinned.

What do the lazy students do for the
school play?
Understudy.

What would you get if you crossed the music department with the school nurse?

A band aid.

Why did the school janitor join the wrestling team?

So he could mop up the floor with his opponent.

What's the hockey team's motto?

"The puck stops here."

What do you call an ice skating goalie who skips school?

A hooky player.

What's the difference between a failing math student and a rabbit?
The rabbit can multiply.

What type of math do pilots study?
Plane geometry.

274

What ballet outfit do math teachers wear?

Two-twos.

Why is arithmetic such hard work?

Because of all the numbers you have to carry.

Why did the ice cream come join the school newspaper?

It knew all the scoops.

Why did Larry and Curly bring their brother to school?

It was Moe-and-tell time.

SCHOOL COUNSELOR: To have self-confidence you must avoid negative words such as "can't" and "not". Do you think you can do that?

STUDENT: I can't see why not.

276

Why did the student think she was aging quickly?

She was told she'd be a senior the next year.

TEACHER: What are you going to be when you grow up?
STUDENT: A soldier.
TEACHER: What if you get killed?
STUDENT: Who would kill me?
TEACHER: The enemy.
STUDENT: Okay, I'll be the enemy.

What is a forum?

Two-um plus two-um.

TEACHER: Tom, what family does the walrus belong to?

TOM: I don't know—no family near us has one.

TEACHER: Larry, do you know what an inkling is?

LARRY: It's a baby fountain pen.

278

TEACHER: Can you use the word "abolished" in a sentence?

STUDENT: Be glad to. "Last night abolished my shoes."

TEACHER: How about "bayou"?

STUDENT: Here goes. "I'll bayou a new skateboard tomorrow."

TEACHER: How about the word "distress"?

STUDENT: All right. "Distress doesn't fit."

Why was the swimming coach fired?
He kept going off the deep end.

Why do dogs go to graduations?
To pick up their masters' degrees.

How was the rowing team
punished?
They were paddled.

Why couldn't the elephant join the swimming team?
It forgot its trunks.

When gym teachers take planes, what class do they travel in?
Coach.

Well, what would you like to do in school this year?
Graduate.

What do you expect to be when you get out of school?
An old man.

Why did the headless horseman go to college?
To join the student body.

Why did the soldiers go to college?
To pick a major.

Why did the quarterback go to college?

To get a passing grade.

What kind of wood is used to build universities?

College boards.

What three R's do cheerleaders have to learn?

"Rah! Rah! Rah!"

Why did the bird-watcher study his throat?

So he could catch a few swallows.

When Eskimos used to trade, they used fish instead of money.

They must have had a hard time getting soda from a machine.

PETE: Have you kept up with your studies?

REPEAT: Yes, but I haven't passed them yet.

How do we know that dolphins are intelligent?

Because it only takes them a few weeks to train a man to throw fish at them.

LITTLE THINGS

What do you get when you cross a vampire with a teacher?

Lots of blood tests.

Why were all the different vegetables angry at the teacher?
She asked them to split off into pears.

How is your cat doing in school?
She's the teacher's pet.

TEACHER: A fool can ask more questions then a wise man can answer.

STUDENT: No wonder so many students flunk your tests.

TEACHER: How do you spell "melancholy"?

STUDENT: The same as everyone else.

TEACHER: What are the five senses?
ROGER: A nickel.

Why were the students in the
boating class so confused?
They were off course.

Why did the washcloth leave the
boxing match?
  Someone threw in the towel.

Why do ghosts go to school?
  To get a dead-ucation.

BOOKS NEVER WRITTEN

Grammar School Is Easy,
by Ella Ment Tree

Making Your Teacher Happy,
by Sid Down

What's New? by I. No

Don't Be a Troublemaker,
by U.B. Goode

STUDENT: What's the capital of Alaska?

TEACHER: Juneau.

STUDENT: If I knew I wouldn't be asking you.

Why did the cow study rocketry?
  To visit the Milky Way.

What was the twins' specialty in baseball?
  The double play.

Why is the school auditorium like a children's toy?
  There's always assembly required.

What assignment do Alaskans bring back from school?
  Nome work.

What did the student say to the calculator?

"I'm counting on you."

What did the circle say to the square?

"I'll be a round."

292

TEACHER: How much water was each sailor in the Spanish Armada allowed to have?
TESSY: I know. Half a galleon.

TEACHER: Name the three zones on the earth?
JENNIFER: Tropic, temperate, and tow-away.

What place in New York do math teachers like?
  Times Square.

TEACHER: Now, class, whenever I ask a question, I want you to answer at once. Doris, how much is six plus three?

DORIS: At once.

Where do track stars keep their valuables?

In a pole vault.

Why did the track team buy CD's?

They were always breaking records.

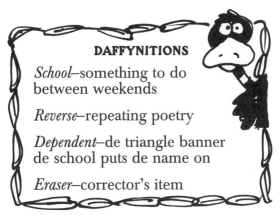

DAFFYNITIONS

School—something to do between weekends

Reverse—repeating poetry

Dependent—de triangle banner de school puts de name on

Eraser—corrector's item

FRED: The basketball coach is
    taking us hunting.
TED: Hunting? Are you sure?
FRED: Yes. He said he were going to
    shoot some hoops.

Why did the track star repave the driveway?

The coach told him to do a little road work.

Why did the giant go to college?

So he could be a big man on campus.

Who does everyone in college confide in?

The Dean of Admissions.

What college courses do veterinarians take?

Baa-ology, Moo-sic, and Pig Latin.

TEACHER: Did the Native Americans
   hunt bear?
THOMAS: Not in the winter.

Why did the wheel get a liberal
education?
   It was well-rounded.

Knock, knock.
Who's there?

Teach.
Teach who?

Teach his own.

TEACHER: The early settlers had many hardships. Name one.
DUFFY: I know one. The wooden Mayflower was a hard ship.

TEACHER: Elizabeth, can you tell me what death is?
ELIZABETH: Patrick Henry's second choice.

CAN WE OPEN A WINDOW? I'M BACON!

TEACHER: Why didn't you answer the question, "Who shot Lincoln?"

STUDENT: Because I'm no squealer.

LITTLE GIRL: What did I learn today?

TEACHER: That's an odd question.

LITTLE GIRL: I know, but that's what they ask me when I get home.

TEACHER: Can you tell me what a myth is?

WILLIE: A female moth.

TEACHER: There are many different species of birds. George, what kind of bird do you like best?

GEORGE: Fried chicken.

That last joke made as much sense as a bird in flight school.

Why don't peaches like school?
They say it's the pits.

Why did the student take sour
cream to the swimming pool?
He wanted to take a dip in the pool.

302

Who arrested the tennis team?
The racket squad.

Why did the tennis player bring a
tray to practice?
It was his turn to serve.

What did the tennis team write for
the school paper?
A love story.

TOM SWIFTIES

"My new word processor has
many typefaces," Tom said
boldly.

Is your teacher strict?
I don't know. I'm too scared to ask.

What happened when the dog went to school?
It had a ruff time.

TEACHER: Why aren't you going
   home from school?
STUDENT: My mother told me not to
   leave school until I graduate.

BOOKS NEVER WRITTEN

How I Improved My Vocabulary,
by I. Reed Moore

Improve Your Reading,
by Ken Hardly Reed

Reading Schoolbooks,
by Turner Paige

Late for School, by I. Bluitt

NED: What did the teacher think of your idea?

TED: She took it like a lamb.

NED: What did she say?

TED: "Baa!"

Why couldn't the flower go to school on its bike?

The pedals were broken.

How did the vampire student start a fire while studying?

By burning the midnight oil.

What happens when a lion goes to school?

Enrollment drops.

TEACHER: Do you know "London Bridge Is Falling Down"?

STUDENT: No, but I hope no one gets hurt.

Why do electric eels go to college?
Because they are so bright.

TEACHER: Will you stop passing notes?
PUPIL: We're not passing notes.
  We're playing cards.

What college is named for John Wayne?
Duke University.

DAFFYNITIONS

Scholarship–a boat of
bright students

Stupendous–advanced
stupidity

TEACHER: Who can give me an
example of a double negative?
PUPIL: I don't know none.
TEACHER: Very good.

Where are army recruits trained?
At private school.

Why did the captain go to college?
For the major.

Why did the navigator want to go away to college?
He wanted to live on compass.

RON: What have all the expeditions to the North Pole accomplished?
DON: Nothing, except they've made geography lessons harder.

QUIET
DOWN

MA: How was your day at school?
SUE: Terrible. I was stung by a
spelling bee.

STUDENT: I'd like to improve my mind by reading.

LIBRARIAN: Would you like something light or heavy?

STUDENT: It doesn't matter. I've got the car outside.

DARREN: If you take away such phrases as "You said it" and "You're telling me" from some people, you can cut their conversation in half.

KAREN: "Don't you know it?"

What must you pay to go to school? *Attention*.

STU: How is your brother doing in college?

PRU: He's halfback.

STU: I mean in his studies.

PRU: Oh, in his studies he's way back.

Why was the football coach nervous during overtime play?

It was sudden death.

Who are the happiest people on the football field?

The cheerleaders.

What did the goalpost say to the football?

"You'll get a kick out of this."

BOOK NEVER WRITTEN

The Successful Football Season, by Owen E. Levin

YOU NEED BRAINS TO TAKE BIOLOGY!...

FRAN: I hear you started to play football.

STAN: Yes. I did it for kicks.

Why are pilots bad at basketball?
They keep traveling.

316

Why did the football coach send in the second string?

To tie up the score.

Why is the playground larger at recess?

Because there are more feet in it.

What kind of candy do kids eat at the school playground?

Recess pieces.

WARPED WISE MAN

School's confusing. I know someone beginning Finnish.

JED: What are you doing in school?

NED: Taking part in a guessing game.

JED: I thought you were taking a test in math.

NED: I am.

318

SON: Did you hear about the new college with an annual tuition of $20,000?

FATHER: What's it called?

SON: IOU.

MAN: I finally stopped my son from going to college late. I bought him a car.

FRIEND: How did that stop him from being late?

MAN: Now he has to get there early to find a parking space.

Why did the art teacher put her
colors on a diet?
  To make the paint thinner.

Why did the math teacher retire?
  His number was up.

320

Why did they stop using the car for driver's ed?

It was retired.

How does a social science teacher break up with his girlfriend?

He tells her she's history.

DAFFYNITIONS

Aftermath–the period following algebra

Serial number–the number you get with milk in the morning

Knock-knock.
Who's there?
Topaz.
Topaz who?
Topaz the text you have to study.

SECOND GRADER: I know the capital of North Carolina.

FIRST GRADER: Really?

SECOND GRADER: No. Raleigh.

Did the teacher really say your singing was heavenly?

No, she said it was unearthly.

How did the science teacher quiz her students?

With test tubes.

What did the chiropractor take at the end of his studies?

A spinal exam.

JANE: I took a book from the library whose cover read *How to Mug*.

MOTHER: What kind of book was it?

JANE: It was volume seven of the encyclopedia.

Why did the book need a chiropractor?
It had a paperback.

Why did the school paper take 365 days to come out?
It wanted to be a yearbook.

THEO: I will never learn to spell.
LEO: Why not?
THEO: The teacher keeps changing the words.

How is a judge like an English teacher?
They both hand out long sentences.

ALPHA-BETTING

$20 ON ELO MENNO P!

JANE: Al is the first person you learn about in school.
WAYNE: Al who?
JANE: Alphabet.

MOTHER: How do you like your new English teacher?

SON: I think she's biased.

MOTHER: What do you mean?

SON: She thinks words can only be spelled one way.

VICTIM: I can't understand how you could have gone to Harvard and still be a cannibal. How can you eat your fellow man?

CANNIBAL: Easy. Now I use a knife and fork.

TOM SWIFTIES

"I forgot my lines in the school play," Tom said speechlessly.

What's a bird's favorite software?
  A seedy ROM.

What do you call a computer
superhero?
  A screen saver.

Where do computers go to dance?
A disk-o.

What animals help run computers?
Rams.

Why were all the computer users
standing in a row?
They were online.

What do you call it when a student
can't answer the questions on
another student's computer test?
Hard copy.

TEACHER: What's your name?
PARENT: Hy.
TEACHER: And what's your son's name?
PARENT: Junior Hy.

Why did the student bring a ladder to school?

He was interested in higher education.

What did the computer component call his son?

A chip off the old block.

TEACHER: What are you doing in the sixth grade, anyway?

STUDENT: I was just going to ask you the same question.

Where did the Cyclops go after the sixth grade?

To junior eye school.

IN AUTOBODY SHOP, WE FIX *TEST TUBES!*

CHEMISTRY TEACHER: Now, should anything go wrong with this experiment the whole laboratory will be blown sky-high. Now stand a little closer students, so you can follow me.

GIRL: You remind me of vacation from school.

BOY: In what way?

GIRL: No class.

If the pilgrims got to America on the Mayflower, how do foreign students get here?

On scholarships.

WARPED WISE MAN
Teachers think the length of a test is like the length of a dress—both should cover the subject thoroughly.

Why did the exchange student take his books on the boat?

So he could study overseas.

Where is Mexico?

On page 10 of the geography book.

334

What do you call the front page of a geography book?

The table of continents.

Why did the Pilgrims wear tall funny hats?

So years later jokes could be made about them in books like this.

TEACHER: What is raised in Brazil during the rainy season?
SALLY: Umbrellas.

Why did Columbus discover America?

So something could happen in 1492.

TEACHER: The African Plains are inhabited by gnus. Michael, can you tell us what's a gnu?

MICHAEL: Not much. What's a gnu with you?

TEACHER: How old will a person be who was born in 1960?

ELLEN: Man or woman?

TEACHER: Where does milk come from?

JAMES: The supermarket.

TEACHER: Tomorrow is groundhog day. Who can tell me what a groundhog is?

JAYNIE: I can. Sausage.

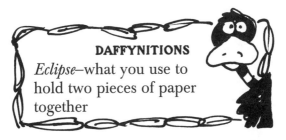

DAFFYNITIONS

Eclipse—what you use to hold two pieces of paper together

Why did the butcher go to medical
school?

He wanted to learn to cure ham.

Where do young cows eat at school?

In the calf-eteria.

Where do math teachers go to eat?
The lunch counter.

Why don't librarians bend the rules?
They play by the book.

TEACHER: What are we talking
about when we say the whole is
greater than the sum of its parts?
STUDENT: A doughnut.

BOOKS NEVER WRITTEN
How to Answer Tough Questions,
by I. Donough
Basic Math, by Adam Upp

FATHER: Stop asking so many questions. Don't you know that curiosity killed the cat?

SON: Really? What did the cat want to know?

CONCERNED STUDENT: Is there life after death?

TEACHER: Why do you ask?

CONCERNED STUDENT: I may need extra time to do my homework.

TEACHER: What's the definition of ignorance?

MORTON: I don't know.

TEACHER: Can you explain inflation?

EILEEN: Every time my father gets a bill he blows up. That's inflation.

When were the Dark Ages?
During the days of the knights.

What did Tiger Woods study at school?

A golf course.

Who are the most athletic boys?

Physical Ed and Jim.

Why did the substitute football player start a fire?

Because the coach told him to warm the bench.

Why didn't the girls' softball team wear stockings?

They had runs in them.

TOM SWIFTIES

"Ball One," Tom shouted in a high-pitched voice.

"I need another baseball glove," Tom admitted.

PLAYER: Our fencing team lost again.
COACH: Ah, foiled again.

Did you hear about the person who cut correspondence school by sending in empty envelopes?

COACH: Why did you show up to the baseball stadium dressed in a suit of armor?

PLAYER: You told me it was a knight game.

SOCCER COACH: Why didn't you stop the ball?

GOALIE: I thought that was what the net was for.

MOTHER: Shouldn't you be doing your homework before going to the playground?

DAUGHTER: I'll let it slide.

TEACHER: Can you define classical music?

ROBERT: Anything without an electric guitar.

Why did the long-distance runner
get good grades?
He was on track.

Why did the track team bring a
steamboat to the gym?
So they could have a tug of war.

Why did the student bring a gate to
the gym?
She wanted to take fencing lessons.

Why did the lazy student think he
could become an astronaut?
*His teacher told him he was taking up
space.*

Is anyone in your class unusual?
Yes; three students have good manners.

Do you go to school?
No, I'm sent.

What do you call a mistake by the entire homeroom?

A class trip.

FRESHMAN: I went to football tryouts yesterday.

FRIEND: Did you make the team?

FRESHMAN: I think so. The coach took one look at me and said, "This is the end."

ABOUT THE AUTHOR

Charles Keller has been working and playing with comedy all his life. Working for CBS as a script consultant, he edited many of the great classic sitcoms, such as *M*A*S*H, All in the Family,* and *The Mary Tyler Moore Show,* and he also worked on other prime-time comedy shows. He got started writing children's books because he didn't like many of the ones he read and thought he could do better. Now, over 50 books later, he maintains the country's largest archive of children's rhymes, riddles, witty sayings, and jokes, and he constantly updates his massive collection. When he isn't writing children's books, he can be found creating educational software for children. Born in New York, Charles Keller is a graduate of St. Peter's College. He presently resides in Union City, New Jersey.

ABOUT THE ILLUSTRATOR

Jeff Sinclair has been drawing cartoons ever since he could hold a pen. He has won several local and national awards for cartooning and humorous illustration. When he is not at his drawing board, he can be found renovating his house and working on a water garden in the backyard. Jeff lives in Vancouver, British Columbia, Canada, with his wife, Karen; son, Brennan; daughter, Conner; and golden Lab, Molly.

Index

356

357